Russia

Tom Streissguth

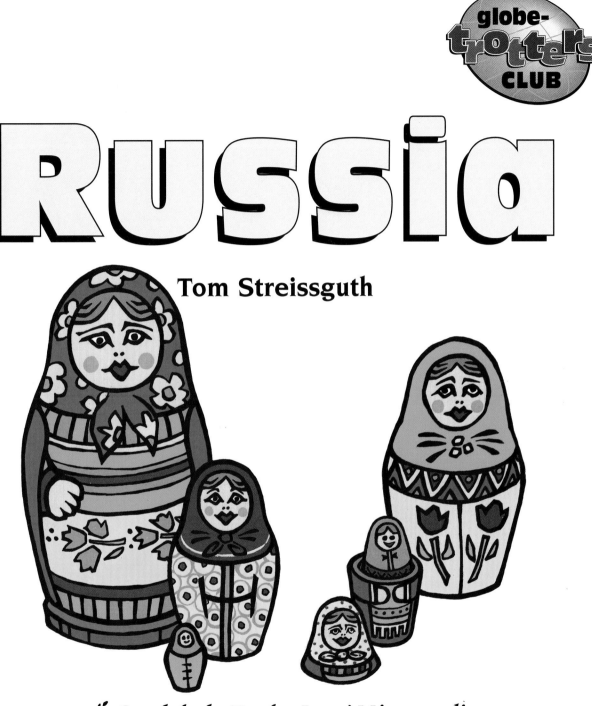

🌿 Carolrhoda Books, Inc. / Minneapolis

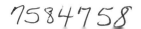

Photo Acknowledgments

Photos, maps, and artworks are used courtesy of: Laura Westlund, pp. 1, 2-3, 4-5, 13, 25, 28, 35, 39, 41; © Wolfgang Kaehler, pp. 4 (inset), 7, 9, 14 (left), 27, 31; © Chris Stowers/Panos Pictures, p. 6; © Dan Buettner, pp. 7 (inset), 8, 10, 11, 14 (top), 17 (bottom), 22 (top), 25, 40; John Erste, pp. 9, 21, 32, 33, 45; Jeff Greenberg, pp. 12-13, 16, 17 (top), 19, 30 (right); Brian Ney, pp. 12 (inset), 28 (left), 44; © Mary Ney, p. 14 (right); © Jean S. Buldain, pp. 14 (center), 30 (left); © Trip/D. Iusupov, p. 15; © Vladimir Pcholkin/FPG International, p. 18 (left); Steve Feinstein, pp. 18 (right), 26 (top); Sovfoto/Eastfoto, pp. 20, 42; Reuters/Bettmann, pp. 21; © Jeremy Hartley/Panos Pictures, p. 22 (bottom); © Trip/D. MacDonald, p. 23; © Trevor Wood/Tony Stone Images, p. 24; Czech News Agency, p.26 (bottom); © Frank S. Balthis, p. 28 (right); Sergej Schachowskoj, p. 29; Corbis-Bettmann, pp. 32 (left and center), 33 (left and center), 37 (bottom); Bettmann Archive, p. 32 (right); UPI/Bettmann, p. 33 (right); Martha Swope © Time Inc., p. 34; Independent Picture Service, p. 35; © Cliff Hollenbeck/Tony Stone Images, p. 36; Reuters/Stringer/Archive Photos, p. 37 (top); © Trip/V. Kolpakov, p. 39; Hollywood Book & Poster, p. 41; John E. Barrett/CTW, p. 43 (top); AP/Wide World Photos, p. 43 (bottom). Cover photo of Kremlin towers © Douglas Armand/Tony Stone Images.

Carolrhoda Books, Inc.
c/o The Lerner Publishing Group
241 First Avenue North
Minneapolis, Minnesota 55401 U.S.A.

Website address: www.lernerbooks.com

Words in **bold type** are explained in a glossary that begins on page 44.

Library of Congress Cataloging-in-Publication Data

Streissguth, Tom, 1958-
    Russia / by Tom Streissguth.
       p.   cm. — (Globe-trotters club)
    Includes index.
    Summary: Examines the topography, society, and culture of the Russian Federation, formerly part of the Soviet Union.
    ISBN 1-57505-101-X (lib. bdg. : alk. paper)
    1. Russia (Federation)-Juvenile literature. [1. Russia (Federation)]
I. Title. II. Series.
DK510.23.S74 1997
947.086-dc21   96-45133

Manufactured in the United States of America
1 2 3 4 5 6 – JR – 02 01 00 99 98 97

Contents

Girls on a tricycle

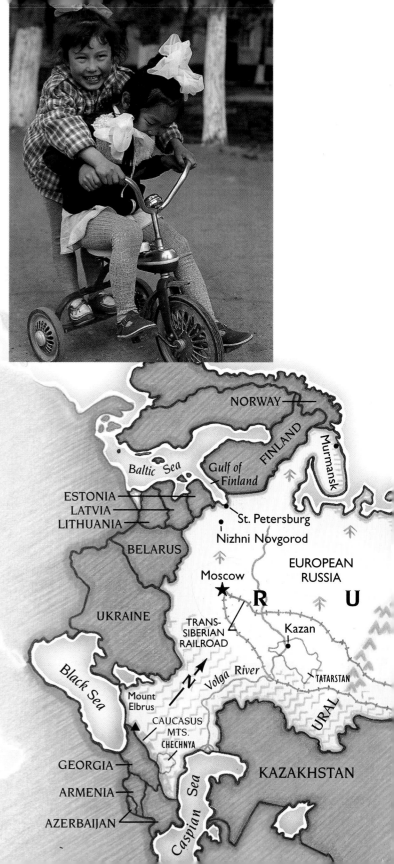

Dobro Pozhalovat
V Rossiyu!*

That's "Welcome to Russia!" in Russian, the official language of Russia.

Russia is the largest country in the world. At one time, Russia was part of an even bigger nation. In 1917 Russia and many of its neighbors became the Soviet Union. The Soviet Union broke up in 1991, and Russia started going by its old name again. From the map, you can see the 13 countries that border Russia.

Russia is on two continents—Europe and Asia. This location sometimes gives Russia a split personality. For example, many of Russia's people and customs are Asian. In the past, Russia's rulers wanted the country to be like Europe. They built buildings and cities to try to make all of Russia *look* European.

NORWAY

FINLAND

Murmansk

Baltic Sea

Gulf of Finland

ESTONIA
LATVIA
LITHUANIA

St. Petersburg

Nizhni Novgorod

BELARUS

Moscow

EUROPEAN RUSSIA

R   U

UKRAINE

TRANS-SIBERIAN RAILROAD

Kazan

Black Sea

Volga River

TATARSTAN

Mount Elbrus

URAL

CAUCASUS MTS.

CHECHNYA

GEORGIA

KAZAKHSTAN

ARMENIA

AZERBAIJAN

Caspian Sea

Party Time

Russia's winters are long, dark, and cold. But in the summer, when the earth tilts toward the sun, the sun's rays cast light over northern Russia all night long. In Russia this time of year is called White Nights. For 10 days in June, the people in the city of St. Petersburg, Russia, celebrate White Nights with music and dancing. People stay up late just to enjoy the natural light.

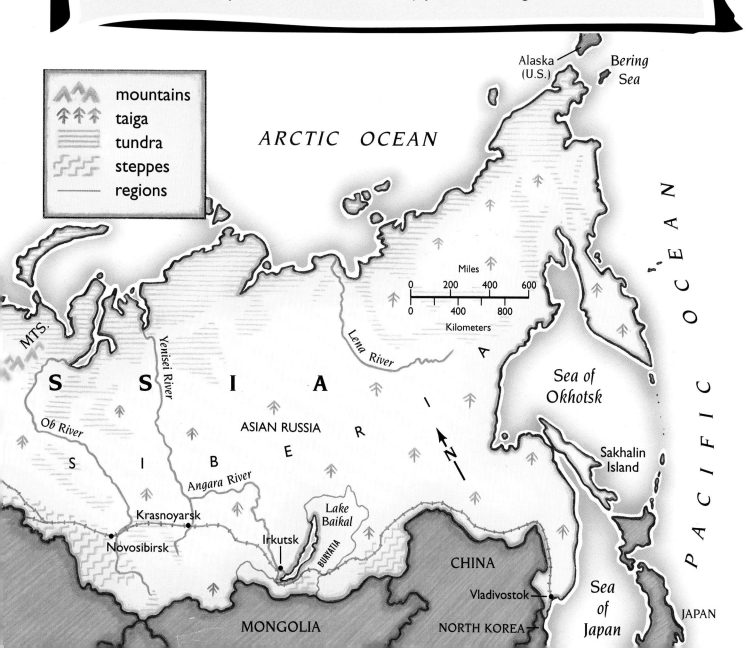

"Bread!" "Blueberries!" "Beets!" shout vendors. At a stop on the Trans-Siberian Railroad, passengers buy food and other goods from people on the platform.

How Big Is
Russia?

 Russia covers 6.6 million square miles in area. That's one-eighth of all the land on our planet! **Siberia,** the biggest section of Russia, lies in the Asian part of the country. There's even a railway line that runs through Siberia. Called the Trans-Siberian Railroad, it takes passengers on a seven-day train ride—the world's longest. The tracks run between the cities of Moscow, Russia's capital, and Vladivostok, on the Pacific Ocean.

Being the biggest country in the world can be tough. Russia has a lot of trees that can be cut down for lumber. But because the country is so large, bringing the wood to places that need it can be costly. Mail is slow, and most Russians don't have telephone service.

Fast Facts about Russia

Name: Russia, or Russian Federation

Area: 6.6 million square miles

Population: 148 million

Major Rivers: Lena, Ob, Volga, Yenisei, Angara

Major Lakes: Lake Baikal, Caspian Sea

Highest Point: Mount Elbrus (18,510 feet)

Lowest Point: coast of the Caspian Sea

Capital City: Moscow

Other Major Cities: Irkutsk, Krasnoyarsk, Nizhni Novgorod, Novosibirsk, St. Petersburg, Vladivostok

Official Language: Russian

Monetary Unit: Ruble

Russian loggers (inset) **cut trees from the vast forests of Siberia. The timber is then loaded onto railcars for transport** (right).

Big *Fun*

The fun thing about being big is that Russia has many different landscapes and a lot of unexplored territory. The highest spot in Russia is Mount Elbrus in the Caucasus Mountains. The peak rises 18,510 feet above sea level.

The Ural Mountains form a border between **European Russia** and **Asian Russia.** On the Asian side of the Urals lies a vast evergreen forest called a **taiga.** The taiga in Russia goes on for more than 3,000 miles, making it the largest evergreen forest in the world. Better wear your long underwear! The forest blankets

(Facing page) **In the summer, wildflowers and tall grasses cover the steppes of Siberia.** (Right) **Evergreen trees from the taiga line a river in Asian Russia.**

Tigers, Bears, and Voles

Northern Russia is like a zoo without barriers for snow-dwelling creatures. Tigers, bears, wolverines, otters, and grouse roam Siberia. These and other animals have found ways to survive in their freezing homes. Field voles (small rodents) burrow underground. The hare and the ptarmigan (a bird) use their snowshoelike feet to walk on top of deep snow. Moose rely on their long legs to stay above the drifts.

Siberia, where winter temperatures can dip to −90°F. The northern part of Siberia is **tundra,** where most of the ground never thaws.

South of the Ural Mountains, wide open fields called **steppes** cover the ground for miles. Farmers plant grains on the steppes, which are not at all like steps. These fields are the flattest plains on earth. Because they're so easy to cross, the steppes were the favorite route for armies and traders traveling between Europe and China.

Lots of Russians live along the winding Volga River. Here a farmer and his son bring in food for their livestock.

Brain Teaser

The Volga is NOT the longest river in Russia but IS the longest river in Europe. Remember that Russia covers parts of Europe and Asia. Russia's longest river, the Lena, flows through Asian Russia.

Water You Looking At?

If you had to build a city, what kind of place would you pick? Worldwide, people have settled where they can support their families, grow crops, and keep animals. All of this adds up to putting cities near water.

Many people live along the Volga River in western Russia. The waterway is 2,325 miles long and runs into the Caspian Sea. For hundreds of years, Russians have used this river to move people and goods. Many cities, dams, power plants, and factories sit along the riverbanks. Barges are a common sight.

Lake Baikal, in southern Siberia, is the world's deepest lake. In some spots, the lake is more than a mile deep. It holds one-fifth of the

Look at the map on pages four and five and try to match up each Russian city with its water source.

Water Matchups

Look at the map on pages four and five and try to match up each Russian city with its water source.

Cities	Waterways
Irkutsk	*Moscow River*
Kazan	*Baltic Sea*
Krasnoyarsk	*Ob River*
Moscow	*Lake Baikal*
Novosibirsk	*Sea of Japan*
St. Petersburg	*Volga River*
Vladivostok	*Yenisei River*

world's freshwater. How did it get to be so big? Part of the answer is that 336 rivers drain into Lake Baikal, while only one flows out!

To spice things up, the Caspian Sea in southern Russia is a saltwater lake. Covering almost 144,000 square miles, the Caspian Sea is the largest inland body of water in the world.

Every summer Siberia warms up enough for its rivers to thaw. At some points, the Lena, the Ob, the Yenisei, and the Angara Rivers spread so wide that a person standing on one bank can't see across to the other side. Oh, remember the one river that flows out of Lake Baikal? It's the Angara.

Lake Baikal sits on an ever-deepening rift, or crack, in the earth's surface.

Getting
Around

 In Moscow the subway is the most common way to travel. It's clean, cheap, and crowded. Many Muscovites (citizens of Moscow) rely on the subway, or underground train, for transportation. Moscow's subway system has 132 stations. One popular stop is Red Square, the largest public square in the world. More and more city dwellers are buying cars. Bicyclists are common in rural areas, but so are horse-drawn carts and people on foot.

The Mayakovskaya station (left) is one of the 132 stops on the Moscow subway system. Passengers getting off at the station near Red Square can visit St. Basil's Cathedral (inset).

Dear Babushka,*

We made it! All the way from Moscow to Vladivostok by train. It took us seven days but it didn't seem so bad. There were two women in our train car whose job was to make sure we had food, sheets, and everything else we needed. Mom says the women are called provodnitsa.

For miles and miles, we saw only grass. When we got to Vladivostok, Dad told me we were near the Sea of Japan! I'll show you on a map when we get home.

Love,

Joseph

*(P.S. That's Grandma in Russian)

All Kinds of **People**

Kids from Sakhalin Island (above)
A retired Russian (right)

Ethnic Russian schoolgirls (above) **and Buryat women** (top)

The people of an **ethnic group** share a language, a religion, and a history. Hundreds of ethnic groups live in Russia. **Ethnic Russians,** the biggest group, are descended from **Slavs,** who lived in eastern Europe thousands of years ago. Russia is split into sections, just as the United States is divided into states. In some areas, the sections are home to mostly one ethnic group.

One part of Russia is called Tatarstan. About 900 years ago, Tatars invaded Russia from central Asia. They battled the Russians and then stayed put. The many-times-great-grandchildren of the Tatar warriors live in Tatarstan. The people in this area speak a language similar to Turkish, the language of Turkey. Most Tatars are Muslims. They follow the religion of Islam.

The Chuvash people make their homes in northern European Russia. They are related to the folks in nearby Finland. In eastern Siberia, the Yakut raise reindeer and horses and try to keep warm. Winters can get as cold as −40°F.

The Aleuts live on the islands just east of mainland Russia. They sail the dangerous Bering Sea. This same ethnic group also lives in Alaska, 50 miles across the water.

The Buryat people live on the shores of Lake Baikal. They have made their homes in Buryatia, the name they give their mountainous region, for hundreds of years.

The traditional clothing of Tatar women includes colorful fabrics and flowing headdresses.

A Long Fight

Chechnya is a small territory in the Caucasus Mountains. The Chechen people farm and own small industries. Many Chechen, however, do not want to be part of Russia. Russians and Chechen have been fighting about this on and off for hundreds of years. In the 1990s, many Chechen were forced to leave their homes to escape warfare. In the mid-1990s, the two groups agreed to stop fighting. But they have not yet solved their differences.

Young Russians (left) chat outside their high-rise apartment building in Moscow. Because her house in the countryside has no indoor plumbing, this elderly Russian (facing page) must bring in water for washing and cooking.

Who Lives
Where?

More than 70 percent of Russians live in cities. Many city dwellers rent or own apartments. That's because housing costs a lot and is hard to find. Families who want to move to a better or bigger apartment usually have to put their name on a waiting list. Months or even years pass before the right apartment becomes available.

Moscow, Russia's capital city, is busy, noisy, and crowded. More than eight million people live there. But Russia has other large cities, too. White Nights, when the sun shines very late in the evening, is a famous event in St. Petersburg. Industries are a big part of life in Novosibirsk, and Irkutsk is known as a hub of fur and timber trading.

Russian farmers live in villages, not on farms. They walk or ride to the fields. Most farms are **cooperatives,** meaning that several families share the land and the work. On the

The City That Peter Built

In the 1700s, Peter the Great was the czar, or leader, of Russia. He wanted to build a city that would be the center of art and education in Russia. He picked a spot where the Neva River meets the Baltic Sea. (Neva means "marsh" in Russian, which gives you a clue about what the ground was like.) The river flowed past more than 100 swampy islands. This made construction a nightmare. Peter's workers struggled to build streets, canals, and more than 300 bridges. And that's how St. Petersburg was born.

A ferry on a canal in St. Petersburg

cooperatives, farmers grow grains and potatoes. Families raise vegetables in backyard gardens.

Even with food growing just outside their doors, life can be hard for country Russians. Most homes don't have running water or flush toilets, and most roads aren't paved. In some remote areas, horses pull plows and carts.

17

(Left) **Soldiers pass in front of a huge wall painting during a Soviet-era parade.** (Below) **A banner showing the Soviet leader Vladimir Lenin was also on view.**

Change Can Be **Hard**

 Since 1991 Russians have been trying to accept a new kind of government. Here's the scoop. For hundreds of years, czars ruled Russia. The czars were powerful, wealthy, and came from one family. Most other Russians were poor and miserable.

Then in 1917, some Russians threw out the czars and set up a new government in Moscow. The government took over many neighboring countries and called the new nation the Soviet Union.

For 75 years, Russia was part of the Soviet Union. The Soviet government was Communist. Its main idea was that all people should share the country's wealth. It sounds fair. But many people in Russia were unhappy with what actually happened. They had few choices in their lives and little chance of making conditions better. The government controlled a lot. People, for instance, weren't allowed to own homes and businesses.

In 1991 a lot happened at once. The republics that made up the Soviet Union went back to being independent countries. New leaders structured a new government. With so many changes, Russians struggle to find jobs and the money to start businesses. Times are uncertain and difficult.

Before the Soviet Union broke up, the government set prices for goods. After prices were freed in 1992, this fruit vendor could charge whatever buyers were willing to pay.

Answer This

When Communists ruled the Soviet Union, they renamed many cities, streets, and buildings. In 1991 these locations got their old labels back. What city on the Neva River did the Soviet Union call Leningrad? Hint: It was built by Peter the Great.

Money—Making It, Spending It

 Jobs can be hard to find in Russia. But certain businesses hire a lot of workers. Some of the largest steel mills in the world are in Russia. Other factories in the nation make cars, trucks, and chemicals. Fishers catch sturgeons for their eggs. Salted sturgeon eggs, called caviar, are a delicacy. People in many countries pay a lot of money to eat Russian caviar.

Speaking of food, most Russian families shop for groceries every day. This is partly because they want to cook with fresh foods. It's also because certain items aren't available every day. It's also because home refrigerators are small. It's NOT because it's fun to shop so often.

The central street in Nizhni Novgorod, Russia's third largest city, bustles with shoppers. Nizhni Novgorod has adjusted to the country's economic changes and is a model for other Russian cities.

Shopping in Russia used to be a lot of work. Soviet stores were famous for their long lines. Many stores made shoppers go through three different lines. At the end of the first line, a salesperson took your order for what you wanted to

Muscovites line up to buy bread.

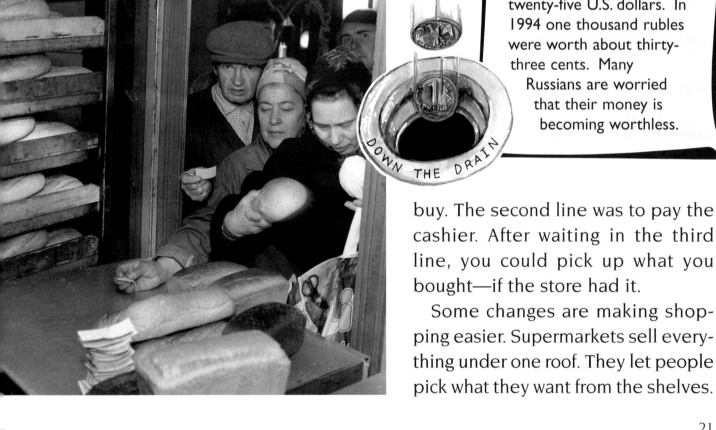

Prices rise quickly in Russia. If you have enough rubles (Russian money) to buy five pencils on Monday, the same amount may buy you only four pencils by the next Friday. In 1993 one thousand Russian rubles were worth about one U.S. dollar. Most Russians earned only twenty-five thousand rubles per month—that's twenty-five U.S. dollars. In 1994 one thousand rubles were worth about thirty-three cents. Many Russians are worried that their money is becoming worthless.

buy. The second line was to pay the cashier. After waiting in the third line, you could pick up what you bought—if the store had it.

Some changes are making shopping easier. Supermarkets sell everything under one roof. They let people pick what they want from the shelves.

21

(Right) **Two brothers and a friend joke around. Is the older brother's gesture familiar?** (Below) **A mother and her children live in one of Moscow's one-room apartments.**

Family Life

Life in modern Russia isn't easy. To make ends meet, both parents typically have to work, if they can both find jobs. The children study hard at school so later on they'll have a chance of getting a good job. Russian women can hold the same jobs as Russian men. They each can be construction workers, doctors, scientists, and mechanics. Both men and women serve in the military.

After a hard day on the job, women do housework and take care of the children. Some grandmothers,

called babushkas in Russian, help watch their grandchildren during the day. Russians respect babushkas and make way for them as they run errands or shop. Grandfathers, or dyedushkas, might help by working in the small gardens that many Russians have.

All in the Family

Russians use the same words as we do to address relatives. Here are the English names, Russian terms, and Russian pronunciations for various family members. Practice them on your own family. See if they understand you!

English	Russian	Pronunciation
father	*atyets*	(ah-TYETS)
mother	*mat'*	(MAHT)
uncle	*dyadya*	(DZYAH-dzyah)
aunt	*tyotya*	(TZYOH-tzyah)
grandfather	*dyedushka*	(DZYAH-doosh-kah)
grandmother	*babushka*	(BAH-boosh-kah)
son	*sin*	(SEHN)
daughter	*doch'*	(DOYCH)
brother	*brat*	(BRAHT)
sister	*syestra*	(seh-STRAH)

Surrounding a bowl of borscht (center) **are other popular Russian foods, including caviar** (on plate with spoon), **hard-boiled eggs, and mushrooms.**

Food for
Thought

Russians are known for their enjoyment of good food and lots of it! For breakfast, they might eat light pancakes, called blini, with sour cream and jam. On special occasions, the blini might even come with caviar.

A Russian dinner usually begins with one or more *zakuski*, or appetizers. A zakuska, served on a large platter, consists of finger foods that everyone at the table shares. While talking about the day's events, the diners nibble on pickles, chopped liver, sliced meats, or cheese. The next course might be borscht, a popular soup that's easy to spot because of its bright red color. The color results from the beets that are in it. The main course usually contains some sort of meat or fish. Beef Stroganoff is a famous Russian meat dish that is popular in Europe and North America, as well as in Russia. Created for and named after a Russian nobleman of the 1800s, beef Stroganoff brings together beef stew and noodles. *Kompot*, a sweet fruit drink, ends the meal.

Make Your Own Zakuska

In the old days in Russia, people often had to travel a long way to visit friends for dinner. The dinner guests might show up one at a time. So the zakuska kept people from getting too hungry!

Here are some ideas for putting together your own zakuska. But you can also use your imagination. Russian cooks often try to arrange the appetizers on the platters in a way that's pleasing to the eye. They might layer the ingredients or roll the meats and cheeses into tubes or make patterns with the vegetables. And remember conversation is a big part of a successful zakuska!

sliced salami and ham	smoked herring	cucumbers, peeled and sliced
cheeses	chopped liver	cherry tomatoes, halved
radishes	dill pickles	bread rolls

This family has just returned from hunting for *gribi* (wild mushrooms), a special treat that grows in Russian forests.

Can you make out the letters on this soft-drink sign?

A *Secret* **Code**

„Русский язык - лёгкий"

Cyril and his brother Methodius were Christian missionaries who worked among the Slavs.

Does this message look like alphabet soup to you? It's what "Russian is easy" looks like if you spell it using the Russian alphabet. You can thank a man named Cyril, who lived about a thousand years ago, for your confusion. He invented this alphabet, called Cyrillic. (Guess who it's named after?) Only Russian and a

All in a Name

It's no big deal if a Russian doesn't care for his or her name. Russians love to use nicknames. In fact, most Russians have five or six! Alexander, for example, can be called Sascha, Saschka, Saschinka, . . .

Use the alphabet chart to find the sounds in your name. See what your name would look like if you were in Russia.

Аа	a	Рр	r
Бб	b	Сс	c
Вв	v	Тт	t
Гг	g	Уу	u
Дд	d	Фф	f
Ее	e	Хх	kh
Жж	zh	Цц	ts
Зз	z	Чч	ch
Ии	i	Шш	sh
Йй	ih	Щщ	shch
Кк	k	*Ъъ	–
Лл	l	Ыы	y
Мм	m	*Ьь	–
Нн	n	Ээ	e
Оо	o	Юю	yu
Пп	p	Яя	ya

* No English Equivalent

few other languages use the Cyrillic alphabet.

The Cyrillic alphabet has 33 letters. Some of the letters look like those in the Roman alphabet, which is used for English and many other languages. A lot of Cyrillic letters share shapes with the Greek alphabet.

A sign in Cyrillic offers American hot dogs for sale.

Happy
Holidays

(Left) **In a Russian Orthodox church, a young woman lights a candle to remember a loved one.** (Above) **In the Soviet era, Santa went by the name Father Frost.**

Holidays are making a comeback! Many traditional holidays in Russia are linked to the country's main religions—Russian Orthodox Christianity, Islam, and Judaism. But in the Soviet Union, openly practicing your religion somtimes got you fired or kicked out of school. Many people chose not to celebrate. After the breakup of the Soviet Union, some folks learned how to observe their holidays for the first time.

The Russian Orthodox religion has holidays throughout the year. This religion, which most ethnic Russians follow, honors a different saint almost every day. Russian Orthodox Christians celebrate their name day—the day of the saint that shares their name—by inviting family and friends to a large dinner.

Easter (Paskha) is the most important Orthodox holiday. Families hold feasts in their homes throughout Easter week. They make a special sweet bread called *kulich* that is shaped like a coffee can. People exchange decorated eggs during Paskha.

Ramadan, an Islamic holiday, draws Muslims together for prayer and fasting. In fact, they do not eat from sunrise to sunset for one month. Jews observe Yom Kippur, their most sacred holy day, every September or October. During Yom Kippur, Jews fast and pray for forgiveness of their sins.

Onions and Basil

Towers topped with onion-shaped domes make Russian Orthodox churches easy to spot. The most famous Russian Orthodox church is St. Basil's Cathedral in Moscow's Red Square. St. Basil's onion-shaped domes are painted in different colors. Each one carries a cross. In the 1500s, the Russian czar Ivan IV (also known as the Terrible!) had the church built to celebrate Russia's victories over the Tatars.

A *School* Day NOT
Like Yours

Beginning at age six, Russian kids spend a lot of time in school. Their only day off is Sunday, and their summer vacation lasts just two months. Students have homework every day. All this work has paid off. Nearly everyone in Russia can read and write.

Teachers in Russia give grades on a scale of one to five. Five is the highest mark. If Russian students don't study enough, they might get a troika. A troika is a sledlike winter vehicle pulled by three horses, so a

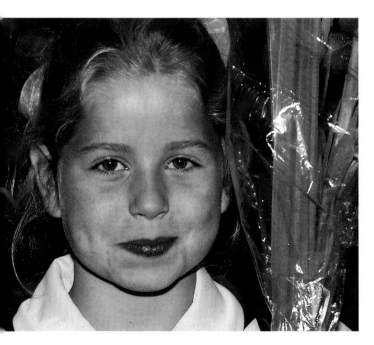

(Left) **On the first day of school, Russian children traditionally bring a flower to their teacher.** (Above) **An older boy helps his younger brother read a book.**

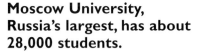
Moscow University, Russia's largest, has about 28,000 students.

troika grade equals a three (an okay mark).

Students study geography, history, math, science, and a foreign language. Many Russians choose to learn English because it's spoken throughout the world. Knowing English gives Russians a better chance of getting a good job when they grow up. Because so many economic changes have taken place in Russia, teachers are also trying to teach their students about the new economy and how it works.

Ninth graders in Russia have a big decision to make. They can enroll in a secondary school with the hope of later taking the exam to get into a university. Or they can go to a vocational school, where they can learn a trade. These schools prepare students for careers in farming or industry.

This trio of great Russian authors—Fyodor Dostoyevsky, Alexander Pushkin, and Leo Tolstoy—wrote before the Soviet era. They are famous worldwide.

Art and **Books**

Hundreds of years ago, Russians began making religious paintings called icons. Icons are almost everywhere in Russia—in churches, in stores, and in people's homes. Some Russians believe that the images can work miracles.

Famous Russian painters include Ilya Repin, who liked to bring to life moments in Russia's history. Marc Chagall, who as a young man left Russia for Paris, has works in public buildings all over the world. Under the Communist government, artists weren't always allowed to paint what they wanted. Some artists left the Soviet Union in protest.

Writers, such as Alexander Solzhenitsyn, were also told what they could and couldn't write about. Since the government changed in 1991, authors have more freedom. Stories by Yevgeny Popov or books by Valery Rasputin are big favorites. Russians also read books by Russian authors who wrote before Communism. They include Alexander Pushkin, Nikolay Gogol, Fyodor Dostoyevsky, and Leo Tolstoy.

The Russian artists **Marc Chagall** (far left) **and Ilya Repin** (center) **had very different styles of painting. Alexander Solzhenitsyn** (far right) **had to leave Russia after writing a book that criticized the Soviet government.**

Watch Out for Baba Yaga

To get a child to behave, a parent may warn him or her of Baba Yaga. Many Russian folktales talk about this old witch who kidnaps and cooks children. They say she lives deep in the forest. The fence around her house is topped with the skulls of children she has eaten. Better be careful. Baba Yaga can change herself into different shapes and sizes.

33

The Greatest
Dancers

Many of the most famous ballet dancers in the world are Russian. Mikhail Baryshnikov, Rudolf Nureyev, and Natalia Makarova are a few who studied in St. Petersburg, a city known for its dance schools. These Russian stars escaped from the Soviet Union, because the government controlled their lives. They left so they could learn other ways of dancing ballet. The choreographer (dance arranger) George Balanchine left St. Petersburg in the 1920s and eventually moved to the United States. Since the breakup of the Soviet Union, choreographers have begun to introduce different forms of ballet in their country.

What a leap! The Russian ballet dancer Mikhail Baryshnikov executes a graceful jump during a performance of _The Nutcracker_.

Basic Ballet

In Russia, as elsewhere, even young children can take ballet classes. At these classes, the students learn to stretch and warm up. Later they train their bodies to do some of the basic steps, or ballet positions. As ballet students grow older—and as their bodies become stronger—they add harder steps and techniques. Most professional ballet dancers have studied and trained for many, many years.

Classical ballet has five basic positions for the feet. You'd see these positions repeated over and over during a classical ballet performance.

Vaslav Nijinksy, a brilliant Russian dancer of the early 1900s, belonged to one of Russia's famous ballet companies—the Ballets Russes. Other important companies that still operate are the Bolshoi Ballet and the Kirov Ballet.

A costumed musician plays the balalaika, the traditional three-stringed instrument designed by the Tatars.

Music to My **Ears**

Hundreds of years ago, Russians and Tatars fought many battles. But Tatars who stayed in Russia gave much to the country's music tradition. Tatars developed the balalaika—a three-stringed instrument heard in most Russian folk songs.

You've probably heard some of the classical music written by Russian composers. A lot of people know *The Nutcracker*, a ballet by Peter Tchaikovsky. Or they may think of *Peter and the Wolf*, written by Sergey Prokofiev. These musical pieces are played by orchestras all over the world.

But if you turn on a radio in Russia, you're most likely to hear Madonna and Michael Jackson. No, they're not Russian. They're just very, very popular.

Michael Jackson performed his first concert in Russia in 1993. Here, fans wait for the singer in front of his hotel in Moscow.

Oh, Just Hum It

Mikhail Glinka

Most countries have a national song, called an anthem, that people sing to show they love their country. In the United States, that tune is "The Star-Spangled Banner."

Russians don't want the Soviet anthem anymore. They have decided to replace it with "Patriotic Song," written in 1833 by a famous composer named Mikhail Glinka. There's only one problem with the song. It doesn't have any words! So Russia is having a contest to see who can write the best lyrics for its new anthem.

Time Out

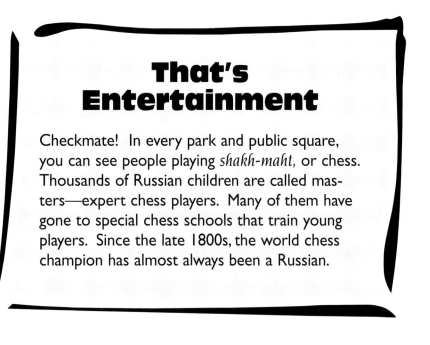

Every city, town, and village in Russia has a soccer field and soccer teams. A professional team called Moscow Spartak competes in European soccer matches.

Winter sports are popular, too, so it's a good thing Russian winters are long. Many people ski cross-country and downhill. Russians do well in ice hockey. Many Russian hockey players have moved to the United States or to Canada to compete on professional teams.

Indoors, Russians bump volleyballs or shoot baskets. Most Russians don't have the money for expensive sports such as tennis and golf. In fact, Moscow has the only golf course in all of Russia.

That's Entertainment

Checkmate! In every park and public square, you can see people playing *shakh-maht*, or chess. Thousands of Russian children are called masters—expert chess players. Many of them have gone to special chess schools that train young players. Since the late 1800s, the world chess champion has almost always been a Russian.

(Facing page) **Cross-country skiers compete in an annual race in Murmansk, a port city that lies in the far northwest along the Arctic Ocean.**

Olympic Success Stories

Russia won 63 medals at the 1996 Summer Olympics, with strong performances in men's gymnastics and men's swimming. Russia also did well at the 1994 Winter Olympics, when for the first time Russian athletes competed for just Russia and not the Soviet Union. Of the 23 medals won in 1994, those for figure skating, speed skating, and the biathlon (skiing and shooting) stand out.

Make mine a quarter-pounder! Hungry Muscovites line up to buy an American-style burger at McDonald's restaurant.

The Wild **West**

For many years, the Communist government wouldn't let Russians see how people lived in the United States and in western Europe. In the late 1980s, large numbers of magazines, television shows, and movies from foreign countries were allowed into Russia. The first McDonald's restaurant in Russia opened in Moscow. Russians began to learn more about "the West."

Since then Russians have been copying some of what they've seen. Some English words have found their way into Russian conversations. Businessmen, for example, are *biznesmen*. A manager is a *meneger*,

During the Cold War—a time when the United States and the Soviet Union were enemies—Russian kids got little real information about the United States. But American kids got a lopsided view of Russia and the Russians, too. The Cold War spies **Boris Badanov** and **Natasha Fatale** (above) are characters from the U.S.-made program, *The Rocky and Bullwinkle Show*.

jeans are *jinzi*, and sneakers (Keds) are *kedi*.

Not all Russians are happy about these changes. During TV commercials, Russian children see ads for candy, toys, and clothes. These products cost more than most parents can afford.

A Warm Front

Since the breakup of the Soviet Union, Russia has made a new friend. For many years the governments of the United States and the Soviet Union did not get along. Their disagreements were so strong it seemed as if they were at war, only there was no combat. Instead of being friendly, the two nations acted coldly toward one another. This behavior was called the Cold War. But since Russia became independent, the Cold War is over.

HOT

COLD

Russians Learning about **Russia**

What's your favorite TV show? The most popular program in Russia is called *600 Seconds*. It covers problems in Russia, including crime, violence, and drugs. Why is it such a hit? The show is popular partly because it pictures real-life stories. Before the 1990s, TV shows in Russia didn't discuss hardships. But Russians want to know the truth about their country, even if some of the news is bad.

Russians like to watch game shows, such as *What? Where? When?* in which players try to stump one another with tough questions.

The Russian Muppets—(left to right) **Kubik, Zeliboba, and Busya**—hold letters from the Cyrillic alphabet.

Russians also like a program called TV *Style*. This late-night show sells clothes, jewelry, and other items. Game shows, talk shows, and Russian movies are popular as well. Viewers can usually find U.S. basketball games and reruns of foreign comedies on air. Preschoolers enjoy *Ulitsa Sezam*—the Russian version of *Sesame Street*. Big Bird is blue and goes by the name of Zeliboba.

Since the end of the Soviet era, Russian television is more free to report on current events. Here, a Russian family watches a speech by Russian president Boris Yeltsin.

Glossary

Asian Russia: The eastern three-quarters of Russia that lie on the Asian continent.

cooperative: A business owned by a group of people who pool their resources, who work together to reduce expenses, and who share the profits of their labor.

ethnic group: A group of people with common characteristics that distinguish the group from most other people of the same society.

ethnic Russian: A descendant of an early Slavic people called Russians who make up the largest ethnic group in Russia.

European Russia: The western one-quarter of Russia that lies on the European continent.

Siberia: A vast region of woodlands, mountains, and plains covering more than five million square miles in northern, southern, and eastern Russia.

Boris Yeltsin and other Russian leaders are depicted on these small dolls.

Slav: A member of an ethnic group that originated in Central Asia and later moved into Russia and eastern Europe.

steppe: A level, treeless plain that dominates the landscape of southern Russia.

taiga: A coniferous (evergreen) forest that covers most of Siberia.

tundra: An arctic region of treeless plains and permanently frozen soil that crosses the extreme north of Russia.

Space Firsts

In 1961 a Russian named Yuri Gagarin took a very long trip. He became the first person to leave the earth's atmosphere in a spaceship. The Russians were also the first to launch a satellite, an object that circles around the earth. The first satellite was called *Sputnik*, which means "traveling companion." The world's first woman astronaut, Valentina Tereshkova, was also Russian. But the very first space traveler was a Russian dog named Laika.

Pronunciation Guide

Baikal	by-CAHL
balalaika	bah-luh-LY-kuh
blini	blee-NEE
borscht	BOORSHT
Buryatia	bur-YAY-shyah
caviar	KAH-vee-ahr
czar	ZAHR
Caucasus	KAW-kuh-suz
Cyrillic	suh-RIHL-ik
Chechnya	CHEHCH-nee-yuh
dobro pozhalovat v Rossiyu	DAH-broh pah-ZHA-lah-vats v'rah-SEE-yu
gribi	gree-BEE
kulich	koo-LEECH
Nizhni Novgorod	NIZ-nee NAHV-guh-rahd
Novosibirsk	no-vo-suh-BURSK
provodnitsa	prah-vahd-NEE-tsah
Siberia	sy-BEER-ee-yuh
Ulitsa Sezam	oo-LEE-tzah say-ZAHM
Ural	YOOR-uhl
Vladivostok	vla-duh-vuh-STAHK
Yenisei	yeh-nuh-SAY

Further Reading

Buettner, Dan. *Sovietrek: A Journey by Bicycle across Russia*. Minneapolis: Lerner Publications Company, 1994.

Chaney, J.R. *Aleksandr Pushkin: Poet for the People*. Minneapolis: Lerner Publications Company, 1992.

Gray, Bettyanne. *Manya's Story*. Minneapolis: Runestone Press, 1995.

Kendall, Russ. *Russian Girl: Life in an Old Russian Town*. New York: Scholastic, 1994.

Kristy, Davida. *George Balanchine: American Ballet Master*. Minneapolis: Lerner Publications Company, 1996.

Leder, Jane Mersky. *A Russian Jewish Family*. Minneapolis: Lerner Publications Company, 1996.

Lye, Keith. *Passport to Russia*. Danbury, CT: Franklin Watts, Inc., 1996.

Morris, Ann. *Dancing to America*. New York: Dutton, 1994.

Nottingham, Ted. *Chess for Children*. New York: Sterling Publishing Company, 1996.

Plotkin, Gregory and Rita Plotkin. *Cooking the Russian Way*. Minneapolis: Lerner Publications Company, 1986.

Polacco, Patricia. *Babushka Baba Yaga*. New York: Putnam Publishing Group, 1993.

Schomp, Virginia. *Russia: New Freedoms, New Challenges*. New York: Marshall Cavendish, 1995.

Symynkywicz, Jeffrey B. *The Soviet Collapse*. Parsippany, NJ: Silver Burdett Press, 1996.

Metric Conversion Chart

WHEN YOU KNOW:	MULTIPLY BY:	TO FIND:
teaspoon	5.0	milliliters
Tablespoon	15.0	milliliters
cup	0.24	liters
inches	2.54	centimeters
feet	0.3048	meters
miles	1.609	kilometers
square miles	2.59	square kilometers
degrees Fahrenheit	5/9 (after subtracting 32)	degrees Celsius

Index